LOW
HISTAMINE
INTOLERANCE
FOOD LIST

The Complete Guide to HISTAMINE INTOLERANCE

Eating for Healthy and Happier Life

LYSANDRA QUINN

Contact the Author

Thank you for reading my book! I would love to hear from you, whether you have feedback, questions, or just want to share your thoughts. Your feedback means a lot to me and helps me improve as a writer.

Please don't hesitate to reach out to me through

contactmelysandraquinn@gmail.com

I look forward to connecting with my readers and appreciate your support in this literary journey. Your thoughts and comments are valuable to me.

TABLE OF CONTENTS

INTRODUCTION

In the midst of a thunderstorm, as the rain relentlessly pounded against the windowpane and lightning lit up the night sky, I found myself immersed in a revelation that would forever alter the course of my life. It was a tumultuous evening, like nature itself was mirroring the storm within my own being. I sat in my cozy living room, huddled under a warm blanket, clutching a cup of fragrant herbal tea, and gazing out into the darkness. As the raindrops streaked down the glass, I reflected on the extraordinary series of events that had led me to this moment – a moment that would ultimately inspire me to pen the pages of a book on low-histamine foods.

Many years ago, I was living an ordinary life, diligently following my career as a dietician. My passion lay in guiding individuals toward better health through nutrition. My days were filled with consultations, meal planning, and helping people make healthier food choices. Yet, it was an unassuming trip to a remote coastal village that marked the beginning of a remarkable journey, one that would lead me to uncover the hidden treasures of low-histamine foods.

The village was a picturesque haven, nestled against the backdrop of lush green hills that met the azure embrace of the sea. It was a place seemingly untouched by time, where traditions ran deep, and the villagers celebrated the simple joys of life. I had chosen this tranquil destination as an escape from the demands of my bustling career. The village promised solitude, a chance to recharge, and the opportunity to indulge in the simple pleasure of savouring nature's bounty.

One morning, I set off on a leisurely exploration of the village, wandering along its narrow cobblestone streets, and observing the locals going about their daily routines. The air was rich with the scent of sea salt and the faint aroma of freshly baked bread. I couldn't help but be captivated by the quaint charm of it all. However, it was my chance encounter with an elderly fisherman that would set my life on an entirely unexpected course.

As I strolled by the harbor, my attention was drawn to an elderly man in faded overalls, meticulously sorting through his day's catch. His gnarled hands worked with the practiced precision of a lifetime spent at sea. Intrigued, I approached him, curious to learn about the local delicacies and culinary traditions.

The weathered fisherman, who introduced himself as Mateo, had an air of wisdom about him that immediately put me at ease. His eyes, filled with stories of a bygone era, crinkled at the corners as he spoke of the village's culinary heritage. He regaled me with tales of flavourful seafood feasts, aromatic herb gardens, and the locals' unwavering commitment to wholesome, fresh ingredients.

As the conversation unfolded, Mateo began to share a particular secret, one that had been passed down through generations but remained largely unknown to the outside world. He spoke of a unique way of eating that had kept the villagers vibrant and healthy for centuries. It revolved around a curated selection of foods, low in histamine, which they believed not only nourished the body but also enhanced their overall well-being.

Intrigued by this revelation, I spent hours in animated conversation with Mateo, absorbing every morsel of wisdom he had to offer. His words resonated with me, and I was struck by the profound simplicity of this approach to food. Little did I know that this chance encounter with Mateo and his village's culinary wisdom would become the catalyst for a profound transformation in my life.

Upon my return home, I delved deep into the world of low-histamine foods, seeking to understand the science behind it and its potential to improve health. I was astonished to find that histamine intolerance was a largely overlooked condition, with countless individuals suffering silently, much like I had during that fateful stormy night.

In the pages that follow, I will guide you through the intricacies of histamine intolerance and unveil the vast array of low-histamine foods that can become your allies in the journey to better health.

You will discover not only the foods to embrace but also the ones to avoid, as well as invaluable tips and recipes to make your transition to a low-histamine lifestyle as seamless and delicious as possible.

Join me in exploring the remarkable world of low-histamine foods and uncover the transformative power they hold. Let this book be your compass, illuminating a path to a healthier, more vibrant you. The journey begins here, and together, we'll embark on a life-changing odyssey of wellness, understanding, and empowerment.

CHAPTER 1

Histamine Intolerance

Histamine intolerance is a condition characterized by an inability to properly break down and metabolize histamine, a naturally occurring chemical in the body. Histamine is also found in various foods and is released in response to allergens and other triggers. When histamine accumulates in excessive amounts, it can lead to a wide range of symptoms and discomfort.

Causes of Histamine Intolerance:

Enzyme Deficiency: Histamine is normally broken down by an enzyme called diamine oxidase (DAO) in the small intestine. In individuals with histamine intolerance, there may be a deficiency in this enzyme, preventing the effective breakdown of histamine.

Reduced DAO Activity: Various factors, such as genetics, medications, and certain medical conditions, can lead to reduced DAO enzyme activity, making it harder for the body to process histamine.

Excessive Histamine Consumption: Some foods are naturally high in histamine, while others can trigger the release of histamine in the body. Consuming an excess of histamine-rich foods or those that promote histamine release can exacerbate symptoms.

Gastrointestinal Disorders: Conditions like leaky gut syndrome, irritable bowel syndrome (IBS), or inflammatory bowel disease (IBD) can disrupt the intestinal lining and potentially lead to histamine intolerance.

Symptoms of Histamine Intolerance:

The symptoms of histamine intolerance can vary from person to person and may include:

Digestive Issues: Abdominal pain, bloating, diarrhea, and nausea.

Skin Problems: Itchy skin, hives, eczema, and flushing.

Respiratory Symptoms: Sneezing, congestion, runny nose, and asthma-like symptoms.

Headaches: Migraines or tension headaches.

Cardiovascular Symptoms: Rapid heartbeat, low blood pressure, and palpitations.

Generalized Symptoms: Fatigue, anxiety, and brain fog.

Diagnosing Histamine Intolerance:

Diagnosing histamine intolerance can be challenging, as its symptoms overlap with other conditions. To determine if histamine intolerance is the cause of your symptoms, consider the following steps:

Keep a Food Diary: Document your dietary intake and symptoms to identify patterns of histamine-rich foods triggering discomfort.

Elimination Diet: A healthcare provider may recommend an elimination diet to remove high-histamine foods from your diet and monitor symptom improvement.

DAO Enzyme Test: A blood test can measure DAO enzyme levels, helping identify if enzyme deficiency plays a role in your intolerance.

Histamine Challenge Test: In some cases, a histamine challenge test, conducted under medical supervision, can help diagnose histamine intolerance.

CHAPTER 2

Low-Histamine Food Alternatives

Low-Histamine Proteins

Chicken Breast:

Nutritional Information (per 3.5 ounces, cooked):

- Calories: 165
- Protein: 31g
- Fat: 3.6g
- Carbohydrates: 0g

Turkey:

Nutritional Information (per 3.5 ounces, cooked):

- Calories: 135
- Protein: 30g
- Fat: 1g
- Carbohydrates: 0g

Whitefish (e.g., cod, haddock):

Nutritional Information (per 3.5 ounces, cooked):

- Calories: 85
- Protein: 20g
- Fat: 0.7g
- Carbohydrates: 0g

Salmon:

Nutritional Information (per 3.5 ounces, cooked):

- Calories: 206
- Protein: 22g
- Fat: 13.4g
- Carbohydrates: 0g

Tofu:

Nutritional Information (per 3.5 ounces, firm):

- Calories: 144
- Protein: 15g
- Fat: 8g
- Carbohydrates: 3g

Quinoa:

Nutritional Information (per 1 cup, cooked):

- Calories: 220
- Protein: 8g
- Fat: 3.5g
- Carbohydrates: 39g

Lean Beef (e.g., sirloin):

Nutritional Information (per 3.5 ounces, cooked):

- Calories: 250
- Protein: 26g
- Fat: 17g
- Carbohydrates: 0g

Pork Tenderloin:

Nutritional Information (per 3.5 ounces, cooked):

Calories: 143

Protein: 29g

Fat: 2.4g

Carbohydrates: 0g

Eggs:

Nutritional Information (per large egg):

- Calories: 72
- Protein: 6g
- Fat: 5g
- Carbohydrates: 0.6g

Shrimp:

Nutritional Information (per 3.5 ounces, cooked):

- Calories: 99
- Protein: 21g
- Fat: 1.4g
- Carbohydrates: 0g

Low-Histamine Fruits

Apples:

Nutritional Information (per medium apple):

- Calories: 95
- Carbohydrates: 25g
- Fiber: 4g
- Vitamin C: 14% of the Daily Value (DV)

Pears:

Nutritional Information (per medium pear):

- Calories: 102
- Carbohydrates: 27g
- Fiber: 6g
- Vitamin C: 12% of the DV

Blueberries:

Nutritional Information (per 1 cup, fresh):

- Calories: 84
- Carbohydrates: 21g
- Fiber: 3.6g
- Vitamin C: 24% of the DV

Kiwi:

Nutritional Information (per medium kiwi):

- Calories: 61
- Carbohydrates: 15g
- Fiber: 3g
- Vitamin C: 71% of the DV

Papaya:

Nutritional Information (per 1 cup, cubed):

- Calories: 55
- Carbohydrates: 14g
- Fiber: 3g
- Vitamin C: 144% of the DV

Watermelon:

Nutritional Information (per 1 cup, diced):

- Calories: 46
- Carbohydrates: 12g
- Fiber: 0.6g
- Vitamin C: 21% of the DV

Mango:

Nutritional Information (per 1 cup, sliced):

- Calories: 150
- Carbohydrates: 38g
- Fiber: 3g
- Vitamin C: 60% of the DV

Cantaloupe:

Nutritional Information (per 1 cup, diced):

- Calories: 54
- Carbohydrates: 13g
- Fiber: 1.4g
- Vitamin C: 68% of the DV

Grapes (seedless):

Nutritional Information (per 1 cup, seedless):

- Calories: 104
- Carbohydrates: 27g
- Fiber: 1g
- Vitamin C: 27% of the DV

Pineapple:

Nutritional Information (per 1 cup, chunks):

- Calories: 82
- Carbohydrates: 22g
- Fiber: 2.3g
- Vitamin C: 131% of the DV

Low-Histamine Vegetables

Zucchini:

Nutritional Information (per 1 cup, sliced):

- Calories: 20
- Carbohydrates: 4g
- Fiber: 1g
- Vitamin C: 35% of the Daily Value (DV)

Sweet Potatoes:

Nutritional Information (per 1 medium sweet potato, baked):

- Calories: 103
- Carbohydrates: 24g
- Fiber: 4g
- Vitamin A: 438% of the DV

Butternut Squash:

Nutritional Information (per 1 cup, cubed):

- Calories: 63
- Carbohydrates: 16g
- Fiber: 2.8g
- Vitamin A: 297% of the DV

Carrots:

Nutritional Information (per 1 cup, sliced):

- Calories: 50
- Carbohydrates: 12g
- Fiber: 3.6g
- Vitamin A: 428% of the DV

Green Beans:

Nutritional Information (per 1 cup, cooked):

- Calories: 31
- Carbohydrates: 7g
- Fiber: 3.4g
- Vitamin C: 15% of the DV

Spinach:

Nutritional Information (per 1 cup, cooked):

- Calories: 41
- Carbohydrates: 7g
- Fiber: 4g
- Vitamin A: 377% of the DV

Broccoli:

Nutritional Information (per 1 cup, chopped):

- Calories: 55
- Carbohydrates: 11g
- Fiber: 3.7g
- Vitamin C: 135% of the DV

Cucumbers:

Nutritional Information (per 1 cup, sliced):

- Calories: 16
- Carbohydrates: 4g
- Fiber: 0.5g
- Vitamin K: 16% of the DV

Red Bell Peppers:

Nutritional Information (per 1 cup, sliced):

- Calories: 39
- Carbohydrates: 9g
- Fiber: 3g
- Vitamin C: 317% of the DV

Cauliflower:

Nutritional Information (per 1 cup, chopped):

- Calories: 27
- Carbohydrates: 6g
- Fiber: 2.5g
- Vitamin C: 77% of the DV

Low-Histamine Grains and Starches

Rice (White or Brown):

Nutritional Information (per 1 cup, cooked white rice):

- Calories: 205
- Carbohydrates: 45g
- Fiber: 0.6g
- Protein: 4.3g

Oats:

Nutritional Information (per 1 cup, cooked):

- Calories: 166
- Carbohydrates: 33.5g
- Fiber: 4g
- Protein: 5.9g

Quinoa:

Nutritional Information (per 1 cup, cooked):

- Calories: 222
- Carbohydrates: 39g
- Fiber: 5g
- Protein: 8g

Buckwheat:

Nutritional Information (per 1 cup, cooked):

- Calories: 155
- Carbohydrates: 33.5g
- Fiber: 4.5g
- Protein: 5.6g

Potatoes (White or Sweet):

Nutritional Information (per 1 medium, baked):

- Calories (White): 130
- Carbohydrates (White): 30g
- Fiber (White): 3g
- Protein (White): 3g
- Calories (Sweet): 103
- Carbohydrates (Sweet): 24g
- Fiber (Sweet): 3.8g
- Protein (Sweet): 2g

Corn:

Nutritional Information (per 1 cup, cooked):

- Calories: 143
- Carbohydrates: 31g
- Fiber: 3.6g
- Protein: 5g

Millet:

Nutritional Information (per 1 cup, cooked):

- Calories: 207
- Carbohydrates: 41g
- Fiber: 2.3g
- Protein: 6g

Tapioca:

Nutritional Information (per 1 cup, cooked):

- Calories: 177
- Carbohydrates: 45g
- Fiber: 0.2g
- Protein: 0.1g

Amaranth:

Nutritional Information (per 1 cup, cooked):

- Calories: 251
- Carbohydrates: 46g
- Fiber: 5.2g
- Protein: 9.3g

Sorghum:

Nutritional Information (per 1 cup, cooked):

- Calories: 143
- Carbohydrates: 35g
- Fiber: 3.5g
- Protein: 4g

Low-Histamine Dairy Substitutes

Almond Milk (Unsweetened):

Nutritional Information (per 1 cup):

- Calories: 13
- Carbohydrates: 0.6g
- Fat: 1.1g
- Protein: 0.5g
- Calcium: 516mg (51% of the Daily Value, DV)

Coconut Milk (Unsweetened):

Nutritional Information (per 1 cup):

- Calories: 50
- Carbohydrates: 1g
- Fat: 5g
- Protein: 0.5g
- Calcium: 455mg (46% of the DV)

Rice Milk (Unsweetened):

Nutritional Information (per 1 cup):

- Calories: 113
- Carbohydrates: 23g
- Fat: 2.3g
- Protein: 0.3g
- Calcium: 283mg (28% of the DV)

Oat Milk (Unsweetened):

Nutritional Information (per 1 cup):

- Calories: 120
- Carbohydrates: 24g
- Fat: 2.5g
- Protein: 3g
- Calcium: 350mg (35% of the DV)

Hemp Milk (Unsweetened):

Nutritional Information (per 1 cup):

- Calories: 70
- Carbohydrates: 1g
- Fat: 7g
- Protein: 2g
- Calcium: 283mg (28% of the DV)

Cashew Milk (Unsweetened):

Nutritional Information (per 1 cup):

- Calories: 25
- Carbohydrates: 1g
- Fat: 2g
- Protein: 0g
- Calcium: 450mg (45% of the DV)

Soy Milk (Unsweetened):

Nutritional Information (per 1 cup):

- Calories: 80
- Carbohydrates: 4g
- Fat: 4g
- Protein: 7g
- Calcium: 300mg (30% of the DV)

Flax Milk (Unsweetened):

Nutritional Information (per 1 cup):

- Calories: 25
- Carbohydrates: 2g
- Fat: 2g
- Protein: 0g
- Calcium: 300mg (30% of the DV)

Macadamia Milk (Unsweetened):

Nutritional Information (per 1 cup):

- Calories: 50
- Carbohydrates: 1g
- Fat: 5g
- Protein: 1g
- Calcium: 220mg (22% of the DV)

Sunflower Milk (Unsweetened):

Nutritional Information (per 1 cup):

- Calories: 25
- Carbohydrates: 1g
- Fat: 2.5g
- Protein: 1g
- Calcium: 283mg (28% of the DV)

CHAPTER 3

High-Histamine Foods to Avoid

Aged Cheeses (e.g., Gruyere):

Nutritional Information (per 1 ounce):

- Calories: 117
- Protein: 7g
- Fat: 9g
- Carbohydrates: 0.1g

Red Wine:

Nutritional Information (per 5-ounce glass):

- Calories: 125
- Carbohydrates: 3.8g
- Protein: 0.1g
- Fat: 0g

Fermented Soy Products (e.g., Soy Sauce):

Nutritional Information (per 1 tablespoon):

- Calories: 8
- Protein: 1g
- Fat: 0g
- Carbohydrates: 1g

Canned Tuna:

Nutritional Information (per 3 ounces, drained):

- Calories: 99
- Protein: 22g
- Fat: 0.6g
- Carbohydrates: 0g

Smoked Meats (e.g., Pepperoni):

Nutritional Information (per 2 slices):

- Calories: 80
- Protein: 4g
- Fat: 7g
- Carbohydrates: 0g

Vinegar:

Nutritional Information (per 1 tablespoon of balsamic vinegar):

- Calories: 14
- Carbohydrates: 3g
- Protein: 0g
- Fat: 0g

Sour Cream:

Nutritional Information (per 2 tablespoons):

- Calories: 60
- Protein: 0.6g
- Fat: 6g
- Carbohydrates: 1g

Ketchup:

Nutritional Information (per 1 tablespoon):

- Calories: 15
- Carbohydrates: 4g
- Protein: 0.2g
- Fat: 0g

Soy Sauce:

Nutritional Information (per 1 tablespoon):

- Calories: 8
- Protein: 1g
- Fat: 0g
- Carbohydrates: 1g

Dried Fruits (e.g., Raisins):

Nutritional Information (per 1 ounce):

- Calories: 85
- Protein: 1g
- Fat: 0g
- Carbohydrates: 22g

Canned Sardines:

Nutritional Information (per 1 can, drained):

- Calories: 191
- Protein: 22g
- Fat: 10g
- Carbohydrates: 0g

Processed Meats (e.g., Salami):

Nutritional Information (per 1 ounce):

- Calories: 107
- Protein: 5g
- Fat: 9g
- Carbohydrates: 1g

Pickled Vegetables (e.g., Pickles):

Nutritional Information (per 1 medium pickle):

- Calories: 7
- Protein: 0.2g
- Fat: 0.1g
- Carbohydrates: 1.6g

Canned Soups (e.g., Tomato Soup):

Nutritional Information (per 1 cup, canned):

- Calories: 94
- Protein: 1.9g
- Fat: 0.8g
- Carbohydrates: 20g

Avocado:

Nutritional Information (per 1 medium avocado):

- Calories: 234
- Protein: 2.9g
- Fat: 21g
- Carbohydrates: 12g

Beer:

Nutritional Information (per 12-ounce can):

- Calories: 153
- Carbohydrates: 12.6g
- Protein: 1.6g
- Fat: 0g

Canned Tomatoes:

Nutritional Information (per 1 cup):

- Calories: 32
- Protein: 1.5g
- Fat: 0.5g
- Carbohydrates: 7g

Processed Snack Foods (e.g., Potato Chips):

Nutritional Information (per 1 ounce):

- Calories: 152
- Protein: 2g
- Fat: 10g
- Carbohydrates: 15g

Eggplant:

Nutritional Information (per 1 cup, cubed):

- Calories: 35
- Protein: 0.8g
- Fat: 0.2g
- Carbohydrates: 8.6g

Spinach:

Nutritional Information (per 1 cup, cooked):

- Calories: 41
- Protein: 5.4g
- Fat: 1.3g
- Carbohydrates: 6.8g

CONCLUSION

As we reach the conclusion of this journey, I find myself overwhelmed with a profound sense of gratitude and hope. The exploration of low-histamine foods has taken us through a labyrinth of information, culinary delights, and, perhaps most importantly, the revelation of a new path to well-being. I hope you've been as inspired as I have been by this remarkable voyage into the world of histamine intolerance.

Histamine intolerance is not just a medical condition; it's a lens through which we can view our relationship with food, our bodies, and our health. It has allowed us to understand that sometimes, the very foods we consume can have a profound impact on our quality of life. But it has also shown us that there is hope and healing to be found through knowledge, awareness, and the power of choice.

In this book, we've navigated through the complexities of histamine intolerance, learning about its causes, its myriad of symptoms, and the science behind it. We've discovered the low-histamine foods that can offer relief, making it possible for individuals like you to lead vibrant and fulfilling lives.

But the journey doesn't end here; it merely marks a new beginning. Armed with the knowledge and tools you've gained, you can embark on a path to better health, greater vitality, and a deeper understanding of your body's needs. It's my fervent hope that this book serves as a trusted companion in your quest for wellness.

Remember that the power to transform your life lies within you. It's in the choices you make each day, the ingredients you select, and the way you nourish your body. And as you walk this path, know that you are not alone. The community of individuals who have embarked on this journey with you, and the support of healthcare professionals and friends, can provide guidance, encouragement, and strength along the way.

My personal journey, inspired by an encounter with an elderly fisherman in a coastal village, has led me to this moment of sharing with you the incredible world of low-histamine foods. It has become a mission, a purpose, and a labor of love. I've watched countless individuals regain their health and vitality, transforming their lives in ways they never thought possible, and I believe in the potential for you to do the same.

So, as we close the final chapter of this book, I encourage you to embrace the knowledge you've acquired and take the first step on your own transformative journey. Nourish your body with foods that support your well-being, listen to the signals it sends, and treat yourself with the love and care you deserve. Histamine intolerance need not be a burden; it can be a gateway to a brighter, healthier future.

Thank you for accompanying me on this incredible odyssey of wellness and empowerment. May your life be filled with good health, joy, and the fulfillment of your dreams. The power to make it so is within your grasp, and I am confident that your path ahead will be a testament to the remarkable potential of the human spirit.

BONUS

Low Histamine Recipes

Chicken and Rice Soup

Cooking Time: 45 minutes

Serving: 4

Ingredients:

- 1-pound boneless, skinless chicken breasts, cubed
- 1 cup rice
- 4 cups low-histamine chicken broth
- 2 carrots, sliced.
- 2 celery stalks, chopped.
- 1 cup zucchini, diced.
- Salt and pepper to taste

Instructions:

1. In a large pot, combine chicken, rice, and chicken broth.
2. Bring to a boil, then reduce heat and simmer for 30 minutes.
3. Add carrots, celery, and zucchini. Cook until vegetables are tender.
4. Season with salt and pepper.

Nutritional Information (per serving):

Calories: 300

Protein: 25g

Carbohydrates: 34g

Fat: 5g

Fiber: 2g

Grilled Salmon with Quinoa and Steamed Spinach

Cooking Time: 20 minutes

Serving: 2

Ingredients:

- 2 salmon fillets
- 1 cup quinoa
- 2 cups low-histamine chicken broth
- 4 cups fresh spinach
- Olive oil for grilling
- Lemon wedges for garnish

Instructions:

1. Season salmon with salt and pepper. Grill for 5-7 minutes on each side until cooked through.
2. Rinse quinoa and cook in low-histamine chicken broth according to package instructions.
3. Steam spinach until wilted.
4. Serve salmon over quinoa with steamed spinach on the side. Garnish with lemon wedges.

Nutritional Information (per serving):

Calories: 450

Protein: 35g

Carbohydrates: 44g

Fat: 15g

Fiber: 5g

Baked Chicken with Mashed Potatoes and Roasted Green Beans

Cooking Time: 50 minutes

Serving: 4

Ingredients:

- 4 boneless, skinless chicken breasts
- 4 large potatoes peeled and diced.
- 2 cups green beans, trimmed.
- Olive oil
- Salt and pepper to taste

Instructions:

1. Preheat the oven to 375°F (190°C).
2. Place chicken breasts on a baking sheet, drizzle with olive oil, and season with salt and pepper.
3. Bake for 30-35 minutes or until the chicken is cooked through.
4. Boil the potatoes until tender, then mash with a little olive oil.
5. Toss green beans with olive oil, salt, and pepper, and roast for 15 minutes.

6. Serve the chicken with mashed potatoes and roasted green beans.

Nutritional Information (per serving):

Calories: 360

Protein: 30g

Carbohydrates: 35g

Fat: 12g

Fiber: 6g

Salmon and Asparagus Foil Pack

Cooking Time: 20 minutes

Serving: 2

Ingredients:

- 2 salmon fillets
- 1 bunch asparagus, trimmed.
- 1 lemon, sliced.
- 2 cloves garlic, minced.
- Fresh dill (or preferred low-histamine herbs)
- Olive oil
- Salt and pepper to taste

Instructions:

1. Preheat the oven to 400°F (200°C).
2. Place each salmon fillet on a large piece of aluminum foil.
3. Arrange asparagus around the salmon, and top with lemon slices, minced garlic, and dill.
4. Drizzle with olive oil, season with salt and pepper, and fold the foil into packets.
5. Bake for 15-20 minutes.

Nutritional Information (per serving):

Calories: 320

Protein: 32g

Carbohydrates: 10g

Fat: 15g

Fiber: 5g

Turkey and Rice Stuffed Bell Peppers

Cooking Time: 1 hour

Serving: 4

Ingredients:

- 4 bell peppers, any color
- 1 pound ground turkey
- 1 cup cooked rice
- 1 can (14.5 ounces) low-histamine tomato sauce
- 1/2 cup diced zucchini.
- 1/2 cup diced carrots.
- 1/2 cup diced celery.
- Salt and pepper to taste

Instructions:

1. Preheat the oven to 350°F (175°C).
2. Cut the tops off the bell peppers and remove the seeds and membranes.
3. In a skillet, cook ground turkey until browned, then drain excess fat.
4. In a large bowl, combine turkey, cooked rice, diced vegetables, and half of the tomato sauce. Season with salt and pepper.

5. Stuff the bell peppers with the turkey mixture and place them in a baking dish.
6. Pour the remaining tomato sauce over the stuffed peppers.
7. Cover the dish with foil and bake for 45 minutes.
8. Uncover and bake for an additional 15 minutes.

Nutritional Information (per serving):

Calories: 340

Protein: 20g

Carbohydrates: 45g

Fat: 8g

Fiber: 5g

Shrimp Stir-Fry with Vegetables

Cooking Time: 20 minutes

Serving: 2

Ingredients:

- 8 ounces shrimp peeled and deveined.
- 2 cups broccoli florets
- 1 bell pepper, sliced.
- 1 cup snap peas
- 1/4 cup low-histamine stir-fry sauce
- 2 tablespoons olive oil

Instructions:

1. In a wok or large skillet, heat olive oil over high heat.
2. Add shrimp and stir-fry for 2-3 minutes or until they turn pink. Remove shrimp and set aside.
3. Add more oil to the wok if needed, then add broccoli, bell pepper, and snap peas.
4. Stir-fry the vegetables for 5-6 minutes until they are tender-crisp.
5. Return the cooked shrimp to the wok and pour in the stir-fry sauce. Stir-fry for an additional 2 minutes.
6. Serve hot.

Nutritional Information (per serving):

Calories: 280

Protein: 25g

Carbohydrates: 14g

Fat: 14g

Fiber: 4g

Low-Histamine Tofu Scramble

Cooking Time: 20 minutes

Serving: 2

Ingredients:

- 1 package (14 ounces) firm tofu, crumbled.
- 1 cup spinach
- 1/2 cup diced zucchini.
- 1/4 cup diced red bell pepper.
- 1/4 cup diced onion.
- 1 clove garlic, minced.
- 1/2 teaspoon turmeric
- Salt and pepper to taste
- Olive oil for cooking

Instructions:

1. Heat olive oil in a skillet over medium heat.
2. Add diced onion, garlic, and red bell pepper. Sauté for 3-4 minutes until softened.
3. Add crumbled tofu and turmeric. Cook for 5-7 minutes, stirring occasionally.
4. Stir in diced zucchini and cook for an additional 3-4 minutes.
5. Add spinach and cook until wilted.

6. Season with salt and pepper and serve hot.

Nutritional Information (per serving):

Calories: 180

Protein: 15g

Carbohydrates: 7g

Fat: 10g

Fiber: 3g

Low-Histamine Turkey and Vegetable Stir-Fry

Cooking Time: 20 minutes

Serving: 2

Ingredients:

- 8 ounces ground turkey
- 1 cup broccoli florets
- 1/2 cup sliced carrots.
- 1/2 cup sliced zucchini.
- 1/4 cup low-histamine stir-fry sauce
- 2 tablespoons olive oil

Instructions:

1. Heat olive oil in a large skillet or wok over medium-high heat.
2. Add ground turkey and cook until browned, breaking it into crumbles.
3. Add broccoli, carrots, and zucchini to the skillet. Stir-fry for 5-7 minutes until vegetables are tender.
4. Pour in the stir-fry sauce and stir to combine.
5. Cook for an additional 2-3 minutes.
6. Serve hot.

Nutritional Information (per serving):

Calories: 270

Protein: 18g

Carbohydrates: 12g

Fat: 16g

Fiber: 3g

Low-Histamine Turkey and Rice Casserole

Cooking Time: 40 minutes

Serving: 4

Ingredients:

- 1 pound ground turkey
- 2 cups cooked rice.
- 1 cup diced zucchini.
- 1/2 cup diced carrots.
- 1/2 cup diced celery.
- 1/2 cup low-histamine chicken broth
- 1/2 cup coconut milk
- 1/4 cup chopped fresh parsley (or low-histamine herbs)
- Salt and pepper to taste

Instructions:

1. Preheat the oven to 350°F (175°C).
2. In a skillet, cook ground turkey until browned, then drain excess fat.
3. In a large bowl, combine cooked rice, diced vegetables, chicken broth, and coconut milk. Season with salt and pepper.
4. Add the cooked turkey and mix well.

5. Transfer the mixture to a baking dish and bake for 30 minutes.
6. Garnish with chopped parsley and serve.

Nutritional Information (per serving):

Calories: 350

Protein: 20g

Carbohydrates: 35g

Fat: 14g

Fiber: 3g

Low-Histamine Baked Cod with Quinoa and Steamed Spinach

Cooking Time: 30 minutes

Serving: 2

Ingredients:

- 2 cod fillets
- 1 cup quinoa
- 2 cups low-histamine chicken broth
- 4 cups fresh spinach
- Lemon juice
- Olive oil
- Salt and pepper to taste

Instructions:

1. Preheat the oven to 375°F (190°C).
2. Season cod fillets with salt, pepper, and a drizzle of olive oil. Squeeze lemon juice over them.
3. Bake for 15-20 minutes or until the fish flakes easily with a fork.
4. Rinse quinoa and cook in low-histamine chicken broth according to package instructions.
5. Steam spinach until wilted.

6. Serve the baked cod over quinoa with steamed spinach on the side.

Nutritional Information (per serving):

Calories: 280

Protein: 14g

Carbohydrates: 23g

Fat: 14g

Fiber: 3g

Made in the USA
Monee, IL
21 January 2024

52155174R00039